FIRST ON THE MOON

Special Edition

First published in the United States by
Hyperion Books for Children,
a division of the Walt Disney Company
114 Fifth Avenue
New York, NY 10011-5690

1 3 5 7 9 10 8 6 4 2

Library of Congress Cataloging-in-Publication Data

Hehner, Barbara.
First on the moon: what it was like when man landed on the moon / by Barbara Hehner, illustrations by Greg Ruhl.
p.   cm.
Summary: An account of the first moon landing by Apollo 11 in 1969.
ISBN: 0-7868-1407-1

1. Project Apollo (U.S.) — Juvenile literature. 2. Apollo 11 (Spacecraft) — Juvenile literature.
3. Space flight to the moon — Juvenile literature. [1. Project Apollo (U.S.).
2. Apollo 11 (Spacecraft.) 3. Space flight to the moon.] I. Title.
TL789.8,U6A5386 1999
629.45'4'0973 — dc21   98-42651

Produced by
Madison Press Books
40 Madison Avenue
Toronto, Ontario
Canada M5R 2S1

Printed in Italy

FIRST ON THE MOON

What it was like when man landed on the moon

MOON

I WAS THERE BOOK

BY BARBARA HEHNER

Illustrations by Greg Ruhl

Historical consultation by Janice Aldrin Schuss and
Roger D. Launius, Ph.D., NASA Chief Historian

A HYPERION / MADISON PRESS BOOK

"Because of what you have done, the heavens have become a part of man's world...

For one priceless moment in the whole history of man, all the people on this earth are truly one."

President Richard M. Nixon speaking to astronauts
Neil Armstrong and Buzz Aldrin

Liftoff!

On the morning of Wednesday, July 16, 1969, a massive Saturn V rocket stood on the launch pad at Cape Kennedy, Florida, creaking and groaning under the weight of millions of pounds of supercooled fuel. Vapor from the liquid oxygen and hydrogen inside its tanks drifted around the great rocket's sides like smoke. It was the largest rocket ever built, and at the very top, over 300 feet (90 meters) above the ground, was the command module of *Apollo 11*. Inside, astronauts Neil Armstrong, Buzz Aldrin, and Michael Collins checked their controls and instrument panels one last time. The first mission to land humans on the moon was about to begin.

It was just after 9 A.M. but the sun was already beating down on the beaches and roadways around the cape. Nearly one million people had gathered there, in the sweltering heat, to watch the launch. Thousands of invited guests were packed into viewing stands about three miles (five kilometers) away from the launch pad. Millions more were sharing the excitement of *Apollo 11* on television, including an eleven-year-old girl named Jan who lived in a suburb of Houston, Texas, called Nassau Bay. Jan knew more about the *Apollo 11* mission than most of the onlookers gathered in Florida. Her father, Buzz Aldrin, was one of the astronauts going to the moon.

Six weeks before, Jan, her mother, Joan, and her brothers, Andy and Mike, had visited Buzz Aldrin in Florida. He took Jan and her brothers through all the steps he would follow on launch day. Now, sitting in front of the television set, waiting for

(Above) A portrait of the Aldrin family, with Jan at far left and Buzz at far right. (Opposite) Buzz Aldrin gives his daughter a tour of the Saturn V rocket that will take him to the moon.

(Left) Neil Armstrong (left), Michael Collins (middle), and Edwin "Buzz" Aldrin were the astronauts selected for the Apollo 11 mission. (Right) The astronauts spent months rehearsing for the moon landing. The Apollo 11 command and service modules (below right) would be linked in space with the lunar module (below) that would take Armstrong and Aldrin to the moon.

Becoming an Astronaut

The first American astronauts were military test pilots, who had already shown that they were used to the dangers of flight. Astronauts also had to be less than 40 years old, in excellent physical condition, and no taller than 5 feet 11 inches (180 cm), to fit inside the cramped space capsule used for the first American space flights. By the early 1960s, when the three Apollo 11 astronauts were selected, astronauts had to be less than 35 years old, but the height limit was raised to 6 feet (183 cm), as command modules became a little roomier.

the countdown to start, Jan replayed the tour in her head. First, Jan had seen the plain but comfortable crew quarters. This was where her father and the other two astronauts awakened at 4:15 that morning, while she was still asleep in Nassau Bay. After a short medical checkup, Aldrin, Collins, and Armstrong sat down to breakfast. Jan even knew what they ate — steak and eggs, the traditional astronaut meal on launch day. Then the astronauts went down the hall to the suit room, where the pieces of their bulky space suits, boots, helmets, and gloves were

(Right) Buzz Aldrin wearing his helmet and "Snoopy cap." (Above) Neil Armstrong practices collecting samples of moon rocks.

laid out for them. "You know what this looks like to me?" her father had joked when he showed his family this room. "An anatomy lab for robots!"

Jan's favorite part of the space suit had been the "Snoopy cap," named after the flying helmet worn by the Peanuts comic-strip character. This was the

close-fitting headgear that contained the astronauts' earphones and microphones. Over the Snoopy cap they each wore a clear bubble helmet that snapped into a metal neck ring on their suits. Buzz had explained to his children how the space suits would be filled with oxygen before the Apollo astronauts set out for the launch pad. They would

The Space Race

 On April 12, 1961, the Soviet Union became the first country to launch a human, Yuri Gagarin, into orbit. Fearing that the Soviets would soon dominate the earth from space, the United States scrambled to catch up. On May 5, 1961, Alan Shepard became the first American in space. Early the next year, John Glenn orbited the earth. President John F. Kennedy promised that the United States would put a man on the moon before the decade was over.

Yuri Gagarin

John Glenn

not breathe Earth's atmosphere again for eight days.

Jan had seen her father and the other astronauts on television that morning, filmed as they left the building just before 6:00 A.M. They walked stiffly in their space suits, each waving to well-wishers with one gloved hand. In the other hand each of them lugged what looked like suitcases, but Jan knew they were portable air conditioners. Then the astronauts got into a van and rode to Launch Pad 39A, just as the Aldrin family had done six weeks before.

Jan and her brothers had ridden a cage elevator up the steel service tower. As the wind whistled through the elevator, Jan watched the ground drop

Neil Armstrong leads the way as the fully suited *Apollo 11* team prepares to enter the Saturn V rocket.

away. It's a good thing I'm not afraid of heights! she thought. The children stood with their father on the walkway that led to the command module, thirty-six stories above the ground. From that height, they could see a long way down the Florida coast.

Even though *Apollo 11* was already in place on the launch pad, Jan and her brothers had not been allowed to climb into the command module. However, she knew just what it looked like. Jan had been inside the spacecraft simulator in which her father and the other astronauts had practiced for months before their mission. She knew that, as

The Saturn V Rocket

The *Apollo 11* astronauts were launched into space by a three-stage Saturn V rocket. Each section was made up of engines and fuel tanks. As the fuel in each one was used up, it fell away, and the next one took over. The first stage, ❶, was by far the largest, standing 138 feet (43 m) high. Its five powerful engines lifted the rocket 39 miles (62 km) above the earth. Then the five engines of the 82-foot (24-m) second stage, ❷, carried *Apollo 11* to 115 miles (185 km) above the earth. The third stage, ❸, 58 feet (about 18 m) long, was topped by the 3-foot (1 m) long instrument unit and had only one engine. It was fired twice: once to put *Apollo 11* into orbit around the earth and later to take *Apollo 11* out of the earth's orbit and put it on its course to the moon.

Escape tower rocket

Emergency escape tower

Apollo 11 spacecraft — 82 ft (25 m)

Command module

Service module

Instrument unit

STAGE ❸

Lunar module

STAGE ❷

Saturn V rocket — 281 ft (86 m)

STAGE ❶

Rocket casing

Aerodynamic fin

(Left) The rocket waits on the launch pad. (Right) The *Apollo 11* insignia.

APOLLO 11

The Saturn V needed three stages to provide enough power to propel it away from the earth. (Left and inset) The rockets in the first section give off clouds of gas and flames. (Right) Within seconds, the Saturn V has cleared the tower. (Opposite left) Minutes later, the first stage, its fuel burned up, drops away.

liftoff approached, all three astronauts were strapped into their seats, lying on their backs with their feet up and held by clamps. Her father was in the middle seat, right under the hatch, facing an instrument panel packed with lights, gauges, and switches.

Jan turned her attention back to the television set. Her mother was sitting quietly beside her now, twisting a handkerchief in her fingers. The countdown was beginning: "T minus fifteen seconds . . . twelve, ten, nine, ignition sequence starts . . . ."

Orange flames and black smoke erupted from the five engines at the base of the Saturn rocket, but it seemed to stand still.

". . . Six, five, four, three, two, one, zero. All engines running. Liftoff! We have liftoff."

Apollo 11 rose slowly beside the tower, as if it were struggling to break away from the earth. "Go, go!" Jan yelled, jumping out of her chair.

The steel arms connecting the rocket to the service tower tore away. *Apollo 11* arced up into the sky, trailing

a blindingly bright column of flame. A thunderous roar rolled over the viewing stands, shaking the ground.

Inside the command module, the noise was muffled. Aldrin thought it sounded like the rumble of a freight train. It was a rough ride for the first few minutes. The astronauts were jerked sharply from side to side as the rocket made automatic corrections in its flight path. Aldrin looked over at Armstrong and saw that he had a tuft of hair sticking out of the front of his Snoopy cap. He looks, Aldrin thought, like a little kid on a toboggan ride.

The sky was so clear that spectators could see the first stage of the Saturn rocket fall away from the spacecraft three minutes and forty-five seconds after liftoff. In that short time, it had already burned more than four and a half million pounds (two million kilograms) of fuel. Less than six minutes later, out of range of viewers and television cameras, the second stage fell away. The rattling and jarring stopped. Aldrin looked down and saw a flap on his space suit floating upward. Then he felt himself lifting off his seat, held only by his safety harness. *Apollo 11* was in orbit around the earth.

The next time Jan saw her father on television, he would be floating weightless in space.

(Left) Jan Aldrin and her brothers Andrew (center) and Michael (right) give their dad the thumbs-up sign after liftoff. (Below) Almost a million people came to Florida to witness the historic launch.

Voyage to the Moon

Apollo 11 made one and a half orbits of the earth, and then the third-stage engines fired automatically. The spacecraft speeded up to 25,000 miles (40,000 kilometers) per hour, fast enough to escape the pull of Earth's gravity.

It was time for the first tricky maneuver of the mission: docking with the lunar module. The lunar module had been stored during the launch at one end of the Saturn rocket's third stage, behind the command module. Now, command-module pilot Michael Collins separated the command module from the third stage. Then, by firing its small jets, he turned the command module around 180 degrees and poked its pointed nose into a doughnut-shaped ring on the lunar module. The astronauts heard a reassuring thump as twelve automatic latches snapped shut, making an airtight seal between the two spacecraft. Now, 50,000 miles (80,000 kilometers) away from Earth, they could finally release the empty third stage of the rocket that had hurled them into space.

Next, Collins adjusted the spacecraft to go through slow rotations side over side like a chicken on a rotisserie. The astronauts called this maneuver "the barbecue roll."

Docking with the Lunar Module

1 The third stage of the Saturn V rocket propels the *Apollo 11* spacecraft toward the moon.

2 The third stage of the rocket opens to free the lunar module. The command and service modules pull away from the third stage of the rocket and begin to make a 180 degree turn.

3 The command and service modules approach the lunar module and position for docking.

4 The command module and the lunar module are now locked together. (Opposite) The third stage of a Saturn V rocket, with the lunar module in place, floats above the earth.

Space Meals

 The food the astronauts took with them into space had to be both nourishing and lightweight. Below are samples of chicken and vegetables, beef hash, and beef and gravy that could be

mixed with water and eaten in space. The astronauts could choose from seventy food items, including dried peaches, shrimp cocktail, potato soup and chicken salad. They could even make instant coffee, but complained that it wasn't "piping hot." To go to the bathroom, the astronauts used a system of tubes and plastic bags.

Every two minutes, the earth disappeared from the window on one side of the spacecraft and reappeared at the window on the other side. The sun followed, shining in the window with a bright hot beam. To Aldrin it seemed like a searchlight, clicking on, clicking off. This roll was crucial. If the spacecraft flew a steady course toward the moon, it would soon overheat on the side toward the sun. The fuel tanks on the hot side would burst, while on the cold side, everything would freeze.

Five hours into the flight, the astronauts were finally able to remove their space suits. Watching everyone struggle out of their suits in cramped quarters, Collins thought they looked like three white whales thrashing in a too-small tank. After the astronauts put on their white jumpsuits, the command

Michael Collins inspects the docking hatch. By opening this hatch, the astronauts could reach the lunar module, now locked together with the command module.

module seemed a little roomier. Aldrin enjoyed the freedom of weightless movement around the command module. However, like the others, he was careful not to make any sudden head movements — that could bring on motion sickness.

All the walls of the command module were covered with little squares of Velcro. Many of the astronauts' supplies had patches of Velcro on them, too. In space, the astronauts could not put a pen or a notebook "down," because it would just float away. Instead, they had to remember to stick things to the wall until they needed them again. Once, they forgot and had to hunt all over the command module for their light meter.

It had been a long time since breakfast, and the astronauts were hungry for their first space meal. The *Apollo 11* menus sounded much like the meals the astronauts might have eaten at home: chicken and rice, pork and scalloped potatoes, or spaghetti and meat sauce, with brownies or butterscotch pudding for dessert. However, most of the main courses had been freeze-dried and packed into plastic containers. Before they could eat, the astronauts had to "cook" their meal by squirting hot water into the containers from a spigot that looked like a water pistol. Aldrin was pleased that they could use spoons to eat. On early space missions, the astronauts had simply squirted tubes of liquid food down their throats.

As their first day in space drew to a close, Aldrin noticed how far away Earth now looked. It was a round disk that fitted easily inside one window frame of the command module. Still, it was very bright: the earth reflects four times as much sunlight as the moon does. There was enough earthshine in the spacecraft to read a book.

Fourteen hours after liftoff, it was time for bed. The astronauts fastened covers over their windows to keep out the circling sun. In the crawl space under the seats, Armstrong and Aldrin zipped themselves into floating hammocks and dozed off. Collins slept on one of the seats, with a lap belt to keep him from floating away.

When they awoke on Day 2 (Thursday), the earth looked no bigger than the dial of Aldrin's watch. The next two days, while *Apollo 11* continued its 240,000-mile (386,000 kilometer) journey to the moon, would be one of the most relaxed parts of the mission. The astronauts had instruments to monitor, experiments to do, and photographs to take, but there was ample time to get everything done.

In fact, life was much more peaceful for Buzz Aldrin than it was for his family back on Earth. Normal life was becoming impossible at the Aldrin house. Friends, neighbors, and relatives bustled in and out at all hours, usually carrying platters and bowls of food. At least, Jan thought, no matter how many visitors filled the house, there was always plenty to eat. She was glad her mother didn't have to worry about cooking.

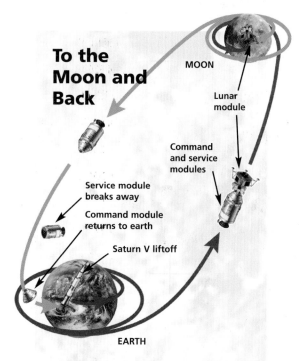

To the Moon and Back

MOON

Lunar module

Command and service modules

Service module breaks away

Command module returns to earth

Saturn V liftoff

EARTH

The powerful engines of the Saturn V lifted the astronauts away from the earth and put them on course for the moon. As they came closer to the lunar surface, the moon's gravity pulled them into orbit around it. The command and service modules orbited around the moon while the lunar module landed on its surface. Since the moon's gravity is not as strong as the earth's, the smaller engines of the service module were powerful enough to take the modules out of orbit around the moon and send them homeward.

Joan Aldrin was too busy greeting people, being interviewed by reporters, and above all, listening to the "squawk box" — a speaker that sat on the divider between the family room and the dining room. This was a direct link to all the transmissions from the Apollo astronauts and Mission Control. Jan tried listening for a while, but she found it hard to tell which voice was her dad's. There was a lot of static and most of the talk was very technical: "Roger, Houston, copy that. Thrust translation, four jets. Balance couple, on. TCA throttle, minimum." An astronaut friend of the family spent many hours at the house, "translating" the transmissions for Jan's mother, so that she could keep track of the mission's progress.

Although there was a flurry of activity inside the house, outside was even crazier. Dozens of reporters were camped out on their street in the blazing summer heat. Whenever Jan and her brothers went for a swim in the backyard pool, television crews and photographers tried to climb over the fence and take pictures of them. Jan thought their behavior was ridiculous. Her father was the one going to the moon; she was just an ordinary kid.

Just before dinner every day, Jan could watch her father on television. The astronauts had been so busy training for their mission that they'd done very little practicing with the television camera. After all, they reasoned, transmitting a jiggly television picture couldn't kill you, while many other mistakes could. Still, when they realized that they were about to broadcast live to two hundred million people back on Earth, they felt a little nervous. They needn't have worried, however — viewers were enthralled by the broadcasts from space.

Jan laughed when her father pointed the television camera out the window and then spun it so that it looked like the Earth was bouncing and rolling in space. "You don't get to do that every day," he joked. Like most viewers, Jan especially enjoyed seeing the astronauts demonstrate weightlessness. "I'm having a great time," her father said, "floating around inside here, back and forth, up to one place and back to another." On Friday afternoon, Aldrin took

(Top) Joan Aldrin answers questions from reporters. (Above) Jan studies a picture of an astronaut. (Opposite) Jan watches a live broadcast of her father from space.

Mission Control

 Launch Control in Florida was responsible for the flight of *Apollo 11* only until it cleared the launch tower. Then direction of the mission passed to Mission Control at the Manned Spacecraft Center in Houston, Texas. There, sitting at banks of computers, engineers and technicians monitored every aspect of the flight, from fuel levels to the astronauts' heart rates. However, then, as today, only one person at Mission Control had direct voice contact with mission astronauts. This was the Capcom (capsule communicator), who was always another astronaut.

television viewers along on an inspection tour of the lunar module. The picture was so clear that it was hard to believe it was coming from more than 170,000 miles (274,000 kilometers) away. Jan was relieved to hear her father say, "Everything looks good down there," as he crawled out of the lunar module. In just two more days, the lunar module would be landing him on the moon.

After Friday's broadcast, Jan decided she needed to get away from the commotion at her house and visit a friend. She grabbed her bicycle and sped off down the circular driveway. As she reached the road, a couple of reporters spotted her and ran after her. "Hey, Jan, wait a minute! Can we just get a quick picture? Are you proud of your dad? How's your mom holding up?" Jan grinned at them over her shoulder, and shook her head. She pedaled faster, until the reporters had to stop, bent over and panting, at the side of the road.

While the astronauts ate breakfast on Saturday morning, darkness swept over their spacecraft. They had flown into the moon's shadow. With the sun blotted out, they could see, for the first time, a sky full of brilliant stars. And when they looked through the window on the other side of the command module, they could see the moon looming, huge and deeply pitted, lit by the ghostly blue light of earthshine.

After lunch, Collins fired the spacecraft's rocket to slow it down enough for the moon's gravity to capture it. *Apollo 11* went

The astronauts orbited the moon thirteen times before separating the lunar module from the command module.

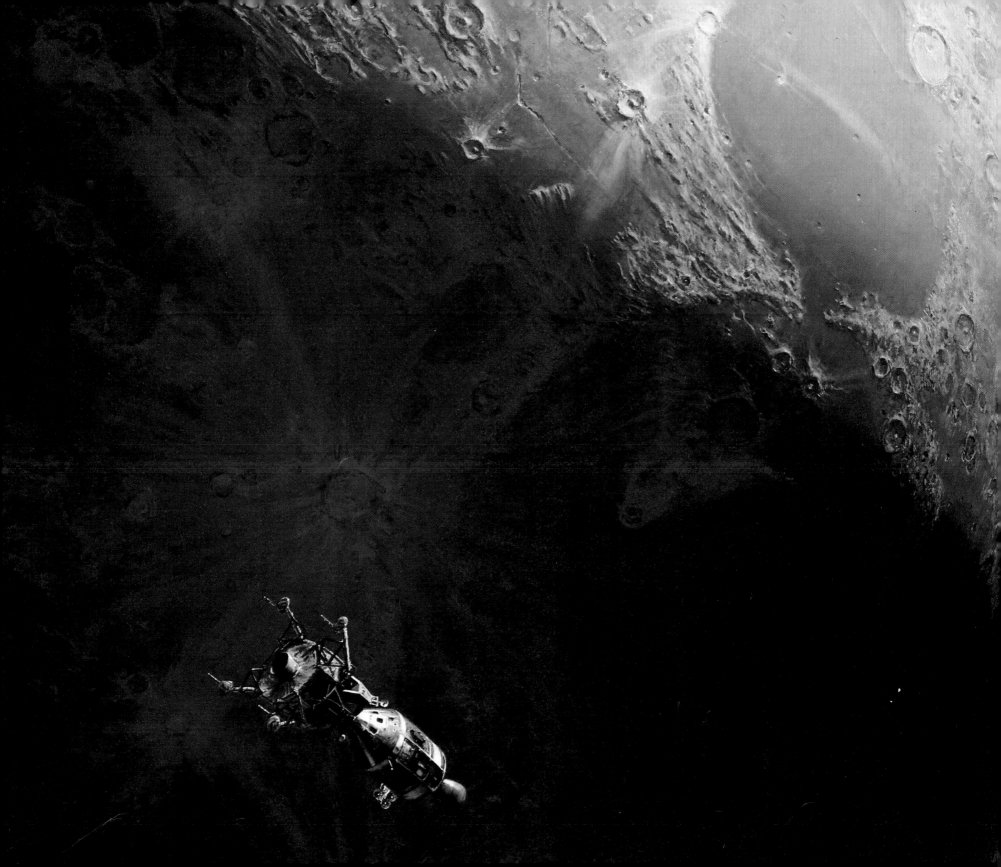

The Face of the Moon

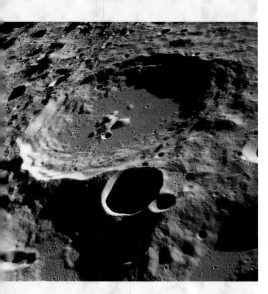

 The moon bears deep scars, called impact craters, from every collision it has ever had with asteroids or meteors. Because there is no air, and therefore no wind, on the moon, any mark made there — even a human footprint — could remain unchanged forever. Unlike the moon, the earth has an atmosphere, which causes most asteroids or meteors to burn up before reaching its surface.

into orbit around the moon, about seventy miles (113 kilometers) above the lunar surface. Every two hours, they made a complete circuit of the moon, and by late afternoon Aldrin was able to spot the place where they were to land the next day. It was called the Sea of Tranquility. But as the astronauts studied it, the area looked craggy and forbidding in the long shadows of lunar dawn. Aldrin told himself that by the time they landed there, with the sun shining on it, the site would appear more welcoming.

Right after breakfast on Day 5 (Sunday), Armstrong and Aldrin donned lunar undersuits with hundreds of fine plastic tubes sewn into them. When they were on the moon, cool water would flow through these tubes, keeping the men from overheating. Then all three astronauts suited up again. This was much more difficult in the cramped quarters of the command module than it had been on Earth. Armstrong and Aldrin squeezed through the connecting tunnel into the lunar module, turned on the electrical power, and checked all the switch settings. Then Collins threw the switch in the command module that disconnected the two spacecraft. Now that

Though Collins did not visit the lunar surface during the *Apollo 11* mission, he had the vital role of piloting the module that would return the astronauts to Earth.

they were separate, the command module would be called *Columbia*, and the lunar module, *Eagle*. While the *Eagle* went to the Sea of Tranquility, Collins would orbit the moon alone.

"The *Eagle* has wings!" Armstrong exclaimed as he worked the controls of the lunar module. But as Collins made a slow tour of inspection around the *Eagle*, he was thinking what an ungainly flying machine it was, with its four spidery legs extended. "Okay, you guys take care," Collins said, as he maneuvered the *Columbia* away from the *Eagle*. "See you later," Armstrong replied. This is it, Aldrin thought. Now it's up to us.

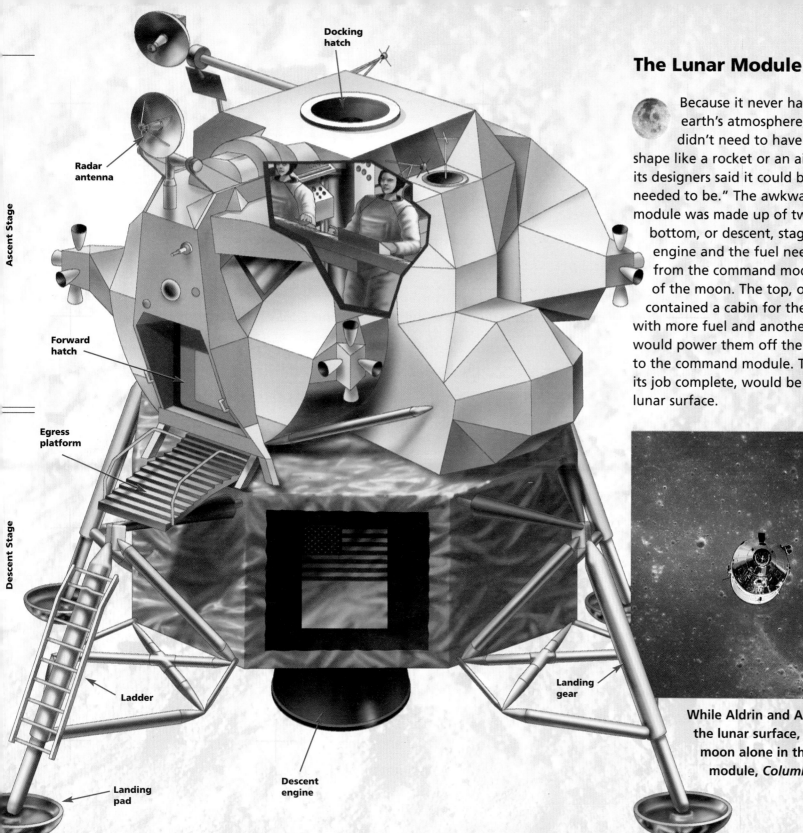

Docking
hatch

Radar
antenna

Ascent Stage

Forward
hatch

Egress
platform

Descent Stage

Ladder

Landing
pad

Descent
engine

Landing
gear

The Lunar Module

Because it never had to fly in the earth's atmosphere, the lunar module didn't need to have a streamlined shape like a rocket or an airplane. One of its designers said it could be "any shape it needed to be." The awkward-looking module was made up of two stages. The bottom, or descent, stage carried an engine and the fuel needed to travel from the command module to the surface of the moon. The top, or ascent, stage contained a cabin for the astronauts, along with more fuel and another rocket, which would power them off the moon and back to the command module. The descent stage, its job complete, would be left behind on the lunar surface.

While Aldrin and Armstrong visited the lunar surface, Collins orbited the moon alone in the command module, *Columbia* (above).

23

"The *Eagle* Has Landed"

The *Eagle* sped toward the surface of the moon at more than 3,000 miles (4,800 kilometers) per hour. Armstrong and Aldrin stood side by side, tethered to the floor by elastic cords. While Armstrong looked out the window and piloted the lunar module, Aldrin kept his eyes on the computer and other onboard instruments. Suddenly, at 3,000 feet (923 meters), warning lights flashed on the control panel, and high-pitched alarms rang in their headsets. But Mission Control quickly informed the astronauts that their computer had become overloaded, trying to process too much data too fast. Nothing was wrong with the lunar module, and it was safe to continue with the landing.

Aldrin kept reading out the data: "Seven hundred feet [210 meters]," he said, giving their altitude above the surface. "Down at twenty-one," he added, meaning they were descending at twenty-one feet (six meters) per second. "Six hundred feet [180 meters], down at nineteen [five meters]."

Armstrong could see the landing site their navigation system was steering them toward, and he didn't like what he saw. A crater the size of a football field was directly in their path, and it was surrounded by boulders, some of them as big as cars. The *Eagle* could be ripped apart if he put it down there. Armstrong took over manual control of the lunar module, slowed down the rate of descent, and skimmed over the crater. As the moon's battered surface loomed closer and closer, Armstrong searched urgently for a better landing spot. Aldrin continued in a steady voice: "One hundred feet [thirty meters], three-and-a-half [one meter] down. Five percent fuel remaining. Quantity light." "Light" meant that they had only sixty seconds of fuel left.

None of Aldrin's practice runs (left) prepared him for the drama of the actual moon landing (opposite).

Out of time, Armstrong finally spotted a flat area and set the *Eagle* down in billowing gusts of moon dust. Armstrong and Aldrin grinned at each other through their bubble helmets, then reached out and shook hands.

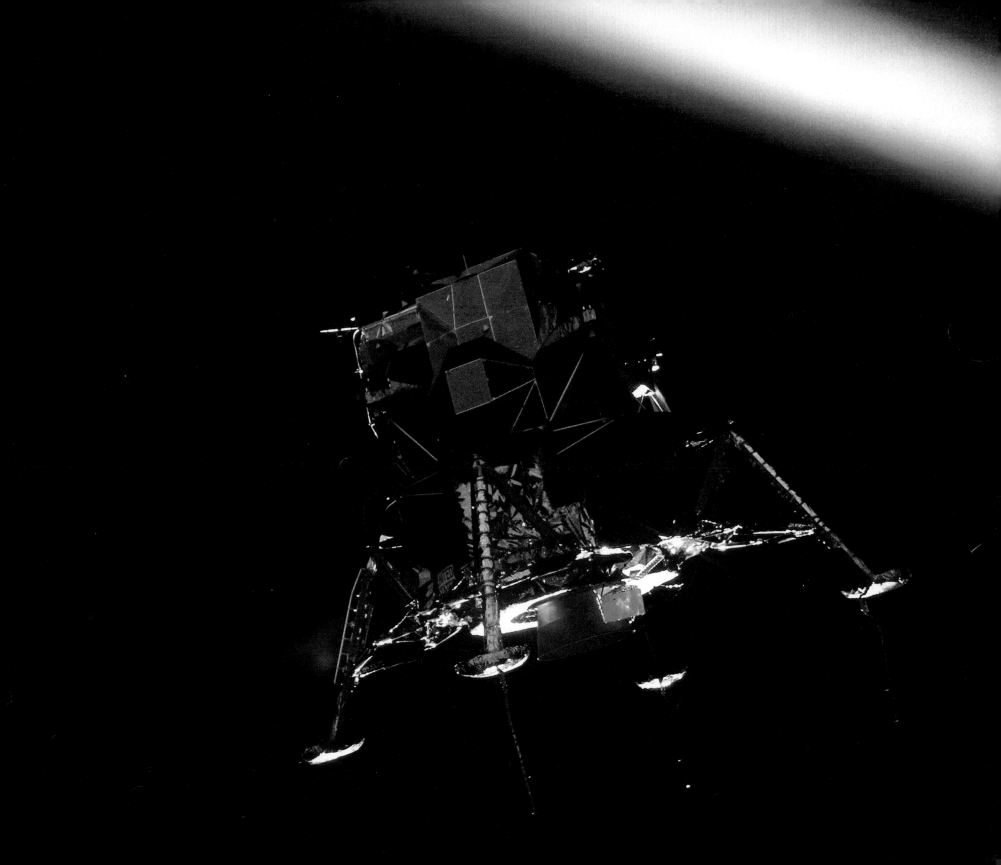

Space Suits

The suits in which Aldrin and Armstrong walked on the moon had over twenty separate layers to protect them from the extreme temperatures on the moon, which could range from -280°F (-173°C) at night to 280°F (138°C) during the day. The outer layer was extra strong to protect them from micro-meteorites. These grains of dust travel through space at such high speeds that they can drill right through an unprotected astronaut's body.

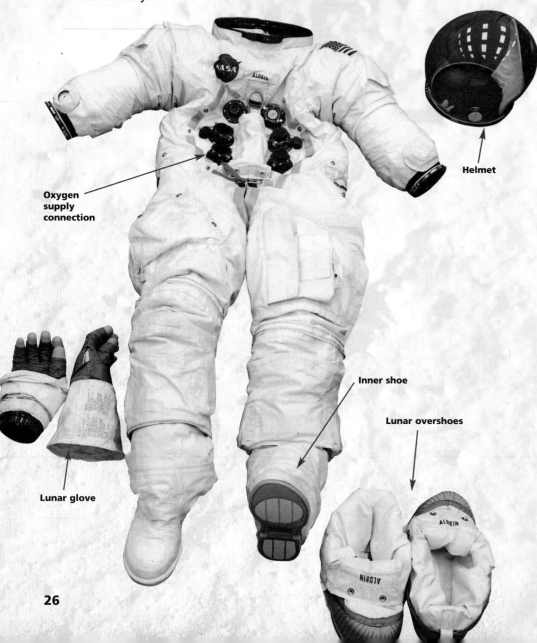

Helmet

Oxygen supply connection

Inner shoe

Lunar overshoes

Lunar glove

Armstrong pushed the button to turn on his microphone: "Houston, Tranquility Base here. The *Eagle* has landed." Mission Control exploded in whoops and cheers.

There were cheers at Jan Aldrin's home in Nassau Bay, too. It was a steamy, rainy afternoon outside, and the house was packed with people — relatives from all over the country, other astronauts with their wives and children, and even a few reporters who had been allowed inside. Everyone had crowded into the family room to watch the Aldrins' only television set. Jan bounced up and down on the sofa in excitement. In just a few hours, she'd see her dad on the moon!

Aldrin and Armstrong gazed in awe at the view from the *Eagle*'s windows: a lifeless plain pitted with small craters and strewn with rocks. Although they were scheduled to take a five-hour rest, both men agreed they wanted to start preparations for their moon walk (officially known as an EVA — Extravehicular Activity) right away. Mission Control gave them the go-ahead.

Suiting up took the astronauts more time than they'd expected. They began by pulling on lunar overshoes with deep treads on the bottom. Then they strapped on their portable life-support systems — the backpacks that would keep them alive on the airless moon. They locked oxygen hoses from the backpacks into metal connectors on the front of their suits. Next, they hooked up the hoses that would carry water from the backpacks through the tubes in their special undersuits. When the astronauts had checked and double-checked all the locks, they put on their moon helmets. These featured gold-tinted visors to protect them from the sun's glare. Finally, they pulled on woven steel gloves that reminded Aldrin of a medieval knight's chain mail.

Six-and-a-half hours after the *Eagle* landed, Aldrin held open the hatch and Armstrong slowly backed out. After pulling on a latch that freed a black-and-white television camera, Armstrong started down the ladder. Millions of people around the world watched as the man in the bulky white space suit hopped off the bottom rung. They heard his voice, peppered with static, say, "That's one small step for a man . . . one giant leap for mankind."

Buzz Aldrin begins his descent from the lunar module.

Moon Rocks

 The Apollo missions brought back three kinds of moon rock samples. Basalts are dark lava rocks from ancient lunar volcanoes. Anorthosites are light-colored rocks that resemble the most ancient rocks on Earth. Breccias are rocks formed when the other types were crushed and fused together by meteorite impacts. All the rocks brought back from the moon are between 4.6 and 3 billion years old — about the same age as the oldest rocks on Earth. Most scientists now believe the moon formed from matter broken off the young Earth by a huge impact — perhaps with an object as large as the planet Mars.

Armstrong quickly scooped some soil and rocks into a bag, which he stored in a pocket on the leg of his space suit. Now, even if the moonwalk had to be cut short, they would still have a precious sample to bring back to Earth.

Fifteen minutes later, it was Aldrin's turn to climb slowly down the ladder. By now, it was just after 10 P.M. back in Houston. Jan and her brothers, in their pajamas, had been allowed to stay up late. Through the long hours of waiting for the moonwalk to begin, she had been afraid she would fall asleep. But now she felt wide awake. She went over to the television screen and put her hand on her father's blurry image. She knew how hard he had worked and how long he had waited for this moment — and there he was, on the moon at last.

"Isn't it something? Magnificent sight out here," Armstrong said to Aldrin. "Magnificent desolation," Aldrin replied in an awed voice. He was struck by the starkness of light and shadow on the moon. As far as he could see, the empty landscape was shades of gray and tan. The

(Above) A spectacular view of earthrise from the moon. (Opposite) Aldrin and Armstrong had only a few hours' worth of oxygen to explore the lunar surface.

only bright objects in view had come from Earth: the glittering gold wrappings on the legs of the lunar module and the brilliant white of Armstrong's space suit. And then he turned and saw Earth. Aldrin thought it looked like a beckoning oasis, shining far away in the sky.

But there was very little time simply to look around. Armstrong and Aldrin wouldn't be on the moon long, and they had a busy schedule. Armstrong mounted the television camera on a stand about sixty feet (eighteen meters) from the *Eagle*, so that the world could watch their activities. Then the astronauts unveiled a plaque mounted on one leg of the *Eagle*, to be left behind when they returned to Earth. Armstrong read it aloud:

> **Here men from the planet Earth**
> **first set foot upon the moon**
> **July 1969 A.D.**
> **We came in peace for all mankind.**

Armstrong went to work with a long-handled scoop and collection box, gathering moon rocks. Meanwhile, Aldrin set up a solar wind collector, which looked like a metal foil banner. He would gather it up later. Back on Earth, scientists could check it for any gas particles it had absorbed.

At home in Texas, Jan watched as a fuzzy black-and-white Armstrong and Aldrin planted the American flag on the moon. What she and other viewers didn't know was how much of a struggle it was. The top

layer of lunar soil was too soft to hold the flagpole upright. Underneath, the ground was so hard packed that they could hardly push the flagpole into it. Aldrin was thinking how embarrassing it would be if the flag fell over with the

(Above) Buzz Aldrin poses proudly beside the American flag. (Opposite) Aldrin pushes a tube into the moon's surface to collect a sample of lunar soil. Beside him is the solar wind collector. (Inset) A remote-controlled camera mounted on the lunar module captured this image of the astronauts planting the flag.

whole world watching. But finally they got it steady. In the Aldrin family room, everyone clapped and cheered as Aldrin saluted the flag.

Exploring the Moon

(Opposite) Buzz Aldrin, photographed by Neil Armstrong, unpacks the equipment that the astronauts would need to conduct experiments on the moon. (Right) The seismic station would measure any moonquake activity. (Bottom left) Aldrin follows Armstrong down the ladder to become the second human to step on the moon. (Bottom middle) The astronauts' footprints are visible all around Aldrin as he walks toward the lunar module. (Bottom right) Aldrin works in the eerie light cast by the earth.

Armstrong stood back and snapped one of the most famous photographs ever taken. It shows Buzz Aldrin standing on the moon. But where his face should be, his gold visor reflects back the lunar module and a tiny Armstrong, holding the camera. Because Armstrong was responsible for taking the pictures, almost all of the *Apollo 11* moonwalk photographs are of Aldrin.

Aldrin took a short jog toward the television camera to test how easy it was to move in his space suit. With every step, he bounced into the air, and he could feel an odd, slow-motion delay before he touched down again. On Earth, he could have stopped his run in one step. On the moon, though, he found that it took him three or four steps to come to a halt. His Earth weight, with the big backpack and heavy suit, was 360 pounds (102 kilograms), but here he weighed only sixty pounds (twenty-seven kilograms). "He looks like someone in an old silent movie!" Jan's mother exclaimed, watching his jerky movements.

Gravity on the Moon

 Because it is much smaller than the earth, the moon's gravitational pull — the force that draws objects toward it — is much weaker than Earth's. Astronauts walking on the moon weigh only one-sixth of their Earth weight.

While Aldrin was experimenting with different ways of moving, word came from Mission Control that the president of the United States was calling. Armstrong and Aldrin stood in front of the television camera to receive congratulations from President Richard Nixon. Then they turned back to their work.

Armstrong and Aldrin had always known that, as the first humans on the moon, they could not spend a long time on the surface. Others would come after them who would continue the work. But it was frustrating to see the moon's wonders laid out before them, and not be able to spend more time investigating them. They couldn't even kneel down to get a close look at interesting rocks, because their space

suits were too stiff. Although Armstrong noticed that some small craters seemed to have something shiny at the bottom, which reminded him of blobs of molten solder, he could not collect samples. The astronauts wished they could explore the giant crater they had passed over when they landed, but their time on the moon was almost up.

Two hours and thirty-one minutes after they had first opened the hatch, Armstrong and Aldrin reluctantly climbed back into the lunar module and sealed it shut.

(Opposite) A dramatic view of Buzz Aldrin with photographer Armstrong and the lunar module reflected in his visor. (Left) The remote camera sent images of the astronauts to Mission Control. Armstrong (top right) and Aldrin (bottom right) snapped each other's pictures aboard the lunar module.

As soon as they took off their helmets, they noticed a sharp odor, "like ashes in a fireplace." It was something no one had ever smelled before: the gritty moon dust that coated their space suits.

Going Home

Twenty-one hours and thirty-seven minutes had passed since the *Eagle* touched down on the moon. Neil Armstrong and Buzz Aldrin fired the engine that would lift the top portion of the lunar module — called the ascent stage — off the lunar surface. This was one of the most dangerous moments of the mission. There was no backup for this engine if it failed, and the command module could not land on the moon to rescue them. But they lifted off without a hitch. Millions of people back on Earth breathed a sigh of relief, and so did Michael Collins in the *Columbia*.

Collins had gone around the moon fourteen times while Armstrong and Aldrin made their landing. For forty-eight minutes of each orbit, he was on the far side of the moon. Then he was out of radio contact, more alone than any human had ever been. But he did

(Opposite) With the earth rising in the background, the lunar module, its mission completed, flies toward the command module. Collins (above) later remarked that from the command module's window, the earth looked so small that he could cover it with his thumbnail.

not feel lonely. As he passed smoothly from day into night and back into day again, he found his solitude peaceful and satisfying. Only one fear had troubled him, and he did not speak of it until much later: that he would have to return to Earth without the others.

Four hours after Aldrin and Armstrong lifted off from the Sea of Tranquility, *Columbia* and the *Eagle* closed in for a rendezvous. Armstrong used the lunar module's small thruster jets to maneuver into position near the command module. Then Collins locked the nose of the command module to the ring on top of the lunar module. Armstrong and Aldrin heard the capture latches bang shut above their heads. Suddenly, the two vehicles began to shake and roll. But Collins in his craft and Armstrong in his quickly steadied them. It was the last tense moment for *Apollo 11*.

Return to Earth

One of the most dangerous parts of any space mission is reentering the earth's atmosphere — the layer of air around the planet. Pulled by the earth's gravity, the *Apollo 11* command module reached a speed of 24,243 mph (39,010 kph).

It had to pass through the atmosphere at exactly the right angle. If it hit at too shallow an angle, it could bounce off the earth's atmosphere,

too steep an angle, and it might burn up. During reentry, the *Apollo 11*

astronauts were out of radio contact with Mission Control for a few anxious minutes. It wasn't until Houston heard the astronauts' voices again that they knew the men were safely on their way home.

Collins opened the passageway between the two modules. Armstrong and Aldrin passed through the precious boxes of moon rocks before they came through themselves. Armstrong thought that he and Aldrin, their white suits covered with black moon dust, looked like chimney sweeps. Not wanting to contaminate the command module, they tried to suction off the dust, using a brush attached to one of the lunar module's air hoses. Finally, they crawled through the tunnel for an exuberant reunion with Collins.

Then it was time to cast the *Eagle* loose. It would go into orbit around the moon, perhaps for hundreds of years. Aldrin and Armstrong were sad to see their little spacecraft go, but there was no way to bring it back home. It had no heat shield to keep it from burning up on reentry into the earth's atmosphere.

Seven hours after docking, Collins fired the rockets to escape the moon's gravitational pull and return to Earth. Armstrong and Aldrin were very tired. They had spent a cold, uncomfortable night in the lunar module after their moon-walk, and they'd had little sleep. Now they could relax for the sixty-hour ride home. First, they took a nap, and then, at 9 P.M., they did a television broadcast. Jan saw her father in a playful mood, now that the dangerous work of the mission was complete. He demonstrated how to make a space sandwich, putting ham spread on a slice of bread that was floating in front of him. Collins squirted water from a water gun into his mouth.

On the evening of July 23, the astronauts made a final broadcast from space. Aldrin said, "We've come to the conclusion that this has been far more than three men on a voyage to the moon, more still than the efforts of a nation. We feel that this stands as a symbol of the insatiable curiosity of all mankind to explore the unknown."

As the *Apollo 11* command module neared home, it went faster and faster. Tugged by Earth's gravity, it reached thirty times the speed of sound. Just after noon on July 24, it streaked through the upper

(Left) The three astronauts are helped from the command module by a Navy diver. All four are wearing special isolation suits just in case the astronauts had brought back unknown germs from the moon. (Above) The module is brought aboard the USS *Hornet*.

atmosphere like a flaming meteor, out of radio contact with Earth for a few tense minutes. Then its three parachutes popped open and lowered it gently at twenty-one miles (thirty-four kilometers) per hour into the Pacific Ocean, 950 miles (1,529 km) west of Hawaii. It landed thirteen miles (twenty-one kilometers) from the recovery ship, the carrier *Hornet*.

The Aldrin family room was once again packed with people. Jan, who had never doubted her father would return home safely, was disappointed that the splashdown happened too far from the *Hornet* to be televised. But her mother and the other adults in the room were giddy with relief. To celebrate, they cut into a big cake in the shape of a rocket.

The command module hit the water upside down, but three flotation bags quickly inflated to turn it right side up. A helicopter that had been circling in the recovery area dropped a raft and Navy divers attached it to the command module. When the astronauts opened the hatch, a member of the recovery team quickly passed them special suits called biological isolation garments — BIGs. These outfits were intended to keep the astronauts from spreading any "moon germs" they may have brought back with them. Wearing their drab gray BIGs, with oxygen masks over their faces, the astronauts clambered into the raft. Then the helicopter hoisted them up, one by one.

When the helicopter landed on the deck of the *Hornet*, Jan caught just a brief televised glimpse of her father. He and the other astronauts walked a few steps to a big stainless steel trailer parked on the deck. This would

(Left) **Still in their isolation suits, the astronauts arrive on board the *Hornet*. (Below) President Richard Nixon shares a joke with the astronauts in quarantine. (Opposite) Buzz Aldrin tells Jan about his journey to the moon.**

be their quarantine trailer until they were back in the United States. Jan thought it was too bad that her father had to spend his first three days back on Earth still cooped up in such a small space.

But in the trailer, Aldrin could finally have a shower. After eight days in space, he decided it was the most satisfying shower of his life. Then, freshly shaven and dressed in a comfortable blue flying suit, he and the other astronauts went to the window of the trailer. President Nixon, who had been waiting on the *Hornet*, welcomed them.

When they arrived back in Houston, the astronauts were still not free to go home. The trailer had been flown to Houston on a cargo plane. Then the astronauts were taken to special quarters at the Manned Spacecraft Center, where they had to stay in quarantine for eighteen more days. They were questioned for hours by scientists and other experts about their moon experiences, while all the details were still fresh in their minds. The scientists were on one side of large panes of glass, and they were on the other.

Jan wanted her father to come home. When the shiny trailer rolled out of the huge cargo plane, she had been at Ellington Air Force Base with her mother and brothers to see it. It was late at night, but the hot television lights made it almost as bright as day. She could see her father through the window of the trailer and talk to him by telephone. While he was in quarantine, it was the same: a window and a

telephone. At least the reception room was comfortable, and there were no reporters around trying to eavesdrop on what she was saying. She thought, this is what it must be like to visit somebody in prison.

After a few days, the astronauts themselves felt as if they were prisoners. They had comfortable quarters and an

The astronauts' wives — from left, Pat Collins, Jan Armstrong and Joan Aldrin — were relieved to see their husbands safely back on Earth.

exercise room, but the time dragged. They missed their families. However, they finally watched videotapes of the television coverage of *Apollo 11*. They saw themselves weightless, broadcasting from space, saw themselves loping in slow motion on the moon, saw the crowds of people around the world, gathered in front of their television sets. Aldrin turned to Armstrong and said,

half-seriously, "Neil, we missed the whole thing."

The relatives went home, the reporters melted away, and it was quiet again in the Aldrin house. The only reminder of their extraordinary week was a freezer full of leftover food. One evening, as Jan and her brothers were getting ready for bed, her father walked in the door, as if he'd just come home from an ordinary workday. Jan, Andy, and Mike raced to their father and nearly knocked him over with their hugs. "Did you bring us some moon rocks?" Andy asked. Aldrin explained that not even the astronauts could bring home moon rocks. But, he said, he had managed to get them a little moondust. Jan exclaimed, "Dad, it was so exciting here. It was like a big party all week. It's too bad you missed everything!" Aldrin smiled — that was almost exactly what he had said to Armstrong.

On August 13, 1969, Jan and the rest of her family got up before it was light outside, and dressed in their best clothes. A car waited to take them to Ellington Air Force Base. Along with the two other astronauts and their families, they boarded the most beautiful plane Jan had ever seen — *Air Force One*, the presidential plane. It was going to be a day Jan would remember all her life.

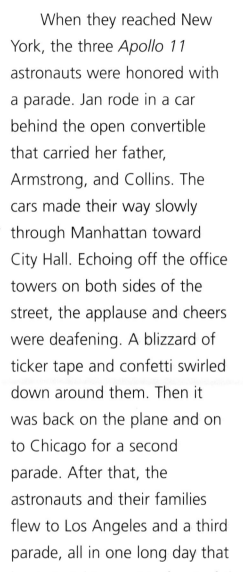

When they reached New York, the three *Apollo 11* astronauts were honored with a parade. Jan rode in a car behind the open convertible that carried her father, Armstrong, and Collins. The cars made their way slowly through Manhattan toward City Hall. Echoing off the office towers on both sides of the street, the applause and cheers were deafening. A blizzard of ticker tape and confetti swirled down around them. Then it was back on the plane and on to Chicago for a second parade. After that, the astronauts and their families flew to Los Angeles and a third parade, all in one long day that kept stretching out in front of them as they traveled west.

The New York ticker tape parade for the astronauts was thought to have been the largest one ever.

In each city, Jan gazed in wonder at the elated faces of the people lining the sidewalk. In Nassau Bay, nearly everyone worked on the space program. It was a normal, everyday thing to have a father who was an astronaut. She had been excited and proud when her father went to the moon, but she had not realized until now that she shared those feelings with thousands, *millions*, of people. They had never met Buzz Aldrin, but they had seen him walk on the moon, and he was their hero.

Epilogue

en more Americans walked on the moon after Neil Armstrong and Buzz Aldrin. All the missions went well, except *Apollo 13*. On that flight, after an explosion in the service module, the astronauts squeezed into the lunar module. It became their lifeboat, looping once around the moon and helping them return safely to Earth. Later Apollo astronauts were able to stay on the moon for several days. *Apollo 15*, *16*, and *17* astronauts

(Above left) Later Apollo missions used lunar rovers to explore even more of the moon's surface. (Above middle) *Skylab*, **launched in 1973, allowed humans to work in space for longer periods of time. (Above right) The space shuttle** *Endeavor*. **(Opposite top left) The orbiting Hubble telescope provides glimpses of the far reaches of outer space. (Opposite bottom left) Jan Aldrin Schuss today with her husband, Larry, and their son, Jeffrey. (Opposite middle left) Today Buzz Aldrin dreams of humans landing on Mars. (Opposite right) The space shuttle** *Challenger*.

explored the moon's highlands and valleys in lunar rovers, lightweight battery-powered vehicles that looked like dune buggies. In all, Apollo lunar missions brought back over 800 pounds (360 kilograms) of moon rocks, which scientists are still studying in their efforts to unlock our solar system's secrets.

The last mission to the moon, *Apollo 17*, took place in December 1972. The mighty Saturn V rocket was used for the last time in 1973 to launch *Skylab*, the first American orbiting space station.

The American space program is now very different from the days of Apollo. Today, women and men of all races, and from many different countries, participate in space shuttle missions. And there are doctors and scientists, as well as military pilots, aboard the shuttle. But the shuttle astronauts go only about 300 miles (483 kilometers) into space, never escaping the earth's gravity; during the Apollo program, humans flew 240,000 miles (386,000 kilometers) to the moon.

Today Jan Aldrin Schuss lives and works in California. She is married and the mother of a little boy. She vividly remembers all the events of July 1969 and the months that followed, when she had to share her father with the world. Jan sees her father often, and he has never lost his enthusiasm for space travel. Buzz Aldrin is active in several organizations that work to encourage space exploration and the building of an international space station. And it is his greatest dream to see human beings on Mars during his lifetime. The license plate on his car says simply: Mars Guy.

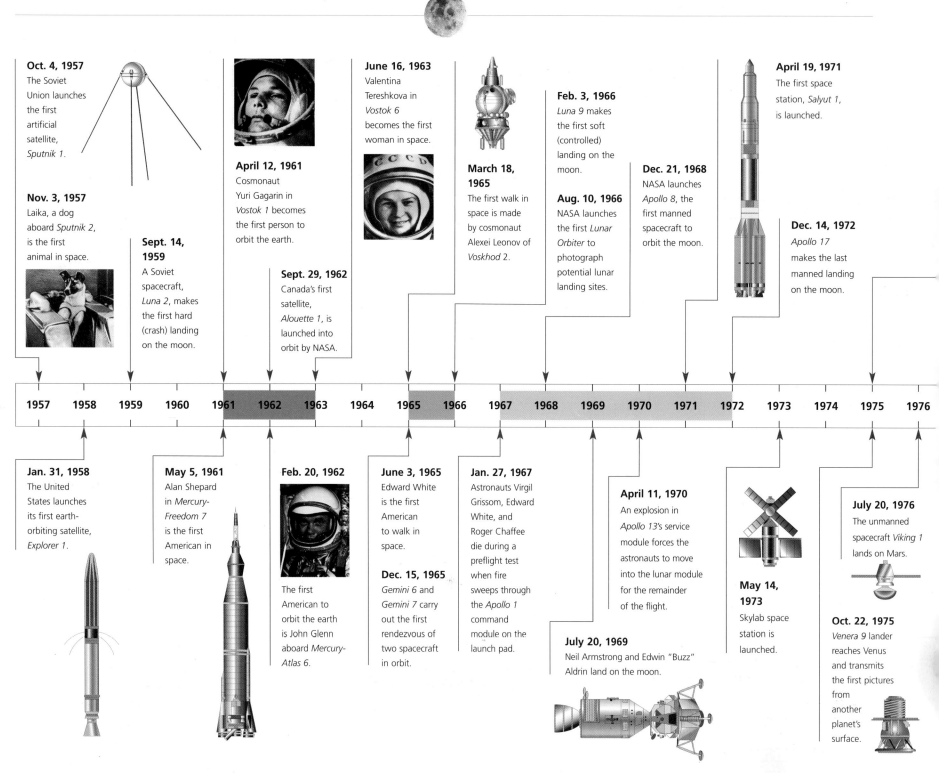

Oct. 4, 1957
The Soviet Union launches the first artificial satellite, *Sputnik 1*.

Nov. 3, 1957
Laika, a dog aboard *Sputnik 2*, is the first animal in space.

Sept. 14, 1959
A Soviet spacecraft, *Luna 2*, makes the first hard (crash) landing on the moon.

April 12, 1961
Cosmonaut Yuri Gagarin in *Vostok 1* becomes the first person to orbit the earth.

Sept. 29, 1962
Canada's first satellite, *Alouette 1*, is launched into orbit by NASA.

June 16, 1963
Valentina Tereshkova in *Vostok 6* becomes the first woman in space.

March 18, 1965
The first walk in space is made by cosmonaut Alexei Leonov of *Voskhod 2*.

Feb. 3, 1966
Luna 9 makes the first soft (controlled) landing on the moon.

Aug. 10, 1966
NASA launches the first *Lunar Orbiter* to photograph potential lunar landing sites.

Dec. 21, 1968
NASA launches *Apollo 8*, the first manned spacecraft to orbit the moon.

April 19, 1971
The first space station, *Salyut 1*, is launched.

Dec. 14, 1972
Apollo 17 makes the last manned landing on the moon.

1957 1958 1959 1960 1961 1962 1963 1964 1965 1966 1967 1968 1969 1970 1971 1972 1973 1974 1975 1976

Jan. 31, 1958
The United States launches its first earth-orbiting satellite, *Explorer 1*.

May 5, 1961
Alan Shepard in *Mercury-Freedom 7* is the first American in space.

Feb. 20, 1962
The first American to orbit the earth is John Glenn aboard *Mercury-Atlas 6*.

June 3, 1965
Edward White is the first American to walk in space.

Dec. 15, 1965
Gemini 6 and *Gemini 7* carry out the first rendezvous of two spacecraft in orbit.

Jan. 27, 1967
Astronauts Virgil Grissom, Edward White, and Roger Chaffee die during a preflight test when fire sweeps through the *Apollo 1* command module on the launch pad.

April 11, 1970
An explosion in *Apollo 13*'s service module forces the astronauts to move into the lunar module for the remainder of the flight.

July 20, 1969
Neil Armstrong and Edwin "Buzz" Aldrin land on the moon.

May 14, 1973
Skylab space station is launched.

July 20, 1976
The unmanned spacecraft *Viking 1* lands on Mars.

Oct. 22, 1975
Venera 9 lander reaches Venus and transmits the first pictures from another planet's surface.

Milestones in Space

July 17, 1975
Apollo 18 and *Soyuz 19* spacecraft dock in orbit.

Sept. 5, 1977
Voyager 1 is launched to explore Jupiter, Saturn, Uranus, and Neptune.

June 13, 1983
The *Pioneer 10* probe is the first man-made object to leave the solar system.

June 18, 1983
Sally Ride becomes the first American woman in space.

July 4, 1997
A *Pathfinder* lands on Mars; 16,550 images are returned to Earth during the mission.

Oct. 29, 1998
Seventy-seven-year-old John Glenn returns to space aboard the shuttle *Discovery*, becoming the oldest man in space.

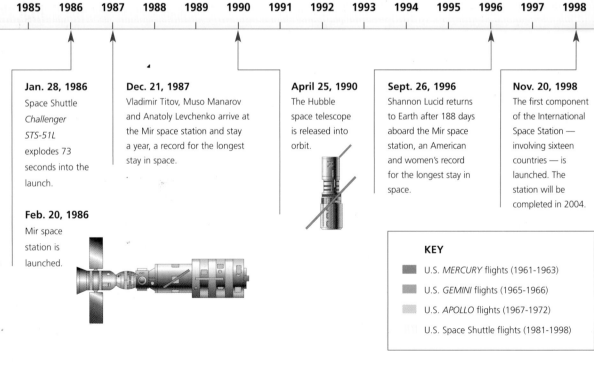

Oct. 5, 1984
Marc Garneau is the first Canadian in space.

July 2, 1985
European Space Agency launches *Giotto* to study Comet Halley.

Jan. 22, 1992
Roberta Bondar becomes the first Canadian woman in space.

1977 1978 1979 1980 1981 1982 1983 1984 1985 1986 1987 1988 1989 1990 1991 1992 1993 1994 1995 1996 1997 1998

Jan. 28, 1986
Space Shuttle *Challenger* STS-51L explodes 73 seconds into the launch.

Dec. 21, 1987
Vladimir Titov, Muso Manarov and Anatoly Levchenko arrive at the Mir space station and stay a year, a record for the longest stay in space.

April 25, 1990
The Hubble space telescope is released into orbit.

Sept. 26, 1996
Shannon Lucid returns to Earth after 188 days aboard the Mir space station, an American and women's record for the longest stay in space.

Nov. 20, 1998
The first component of the International Space Station — involving sixteen countries — is launched. The station will be completed in 2004.

April 12, 1981
Columbia STS-1 is the first airplane-like craft to be launched into orbit.

Nov. 12-14, 1981
The Canadarm Remote Manipulator System is successfully operated for the first time on the second space shuttle flight.

Feb. 20, 1986
Mir space station is launched.

Dec. 24, 1979
Europe enters the space age with the Ariane 1 rocket, used to launch commercial satellites.

KEY

U.S. *MERCURY* flights (1961-1963)

U.S. *GEMINI* flights (1965-1966)

U.S. *APOLLO* flights (1967-1972)

U.S. Space Shuttle flights (1981-1998)

Glossary

command module: The cone-shaped top section of the spacecraft where the astronauts lived during the moon mission.

crater: A pit or hole in the moon's surface formed by the impact of a meteor.

heat shield: A protective coating on the command module that kept the spacecraft cool as it returned to Earth.

liftoff: The takeoff of a rocket from the launch pad.

lunar module: The part of the spacecraft used to carry the astronauts from the command module to the moon.

"That's one small step...": Although Neil Armstrong's famous words are often reported as "That's one small step for man ..." he actually meant to say, "That's one small step for **a** man...."

orbit: The journey of a spacecraft around a planet or moon.

quarantine: The time after the astronauts returned from the moon when they were unable to be in close contact with people in case they had brought back "moon germs."

Sea of Tranquility: A flat plain on the moon's surface; it is not a real sea because there is no water on the moon.

service module: The section of the spacecraft that supplies power, water, oxygen, and electricity to the command module.

solar wind collector: A device used to collect particles from the surface of the sun that are released into space.

splashdown: The landing of a spacecraft in the ocean.

visor: The specially coated front piece of an astronaut's bubble helmet, which protects his eyes while outside the spacecraft.

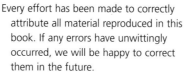

Picture Credits

Every effort has been made to correctly attribute all material reproduced in this book. If any errors have unwittingly occurred, we will be happy to correct them in the future.

All paintings, unless otherwise credited, are by Greg Ruhl.

All photographs, unless otherwise designated, are courtesy of the **National Aeronautics and Space Administration (NASA).**

Front cover: (Top right) Corbis Digital Stock
Back Cover: (Left) *Columbia and Eagle* © 1987 Wilson Hurley, courtesy The Greenwich Workshop Inc.
Pages 4-5: Corbis Digital Stock
Page 7: Collection of Janice Aldrin Schuss
Page 9: (Right) Corbis-Bettmann

Page 10: (Top left and right) UPI/Corbis-Bettmann
Page 11: Diagram by Dan Fell
Page 13: (Middle and bottom) UPI/Corbis-Bettmann
Page 14: Diagram by Dan Fell
Page 15: Corbis Digital Stock
Page 16: (Left) UPI/Corbis-Bettmann
Page 17: Diagram by Dan Fell
Page 19: (Top) UPI/Corbis-Bettmann; (Bottom) Collection of Janice Aldrin Schuss
Page 20: (All) UPI/Corbis-Bettmann
Page 21: *Columbia and Eagle* © 1987 Wilson Hurley, courtesy The Greenwich Workshop Inc.
Page 22: (Left) Corbis Digital Stock; (Right) UPI/Corbis-Bettmann
Page 23: Diagram by Dan Fell
Page 28: (All) Corbis Digital Stock

Page 33: (Bottom left) UPI/Corbis-Bettmann
Page 37: UPI/Corbis-Bettmann
Page 38: Diagram by Dan Fell
Page 44: (All) Corbis Digital Stock
Page 45: (Top left and right) Corbis Digital Stock; (Bottom left and right) Collection of Janice Aldrin Schuss
Page 46: (All photos) UPI/Corbis-Bettmann; Diagrams by Dan Fell
Page 47: Diagrams by Dan Fell

Acknowledgments

Madison Press Books would like to thank Debra Dodds of NASA, for her exceptional speed and cheer when filling picture orders.

Recommended Further Reading

Look Inside Cross Sections: Space

by Moira Butterfield, Illustrated by Nick Lipscombe and Gary Biggin Scholastic/Dorling Kindersley (U.S. and Canada)

● Detailed cross sections of some of the best known spacecraft, including the Apollo lunar and command modules, *Sklylab*, and the Hubble telescope.

Project Apollo

by Diane M. and Paul P. Sipiera Children's Press (A Division of Grolier Publishing) (U.S. and Canada)

● Tells the story of the eleven Apollo flights that sent the first humans to the moon. Complete with useful web sites.

I Want to be an Astronaut

by Catherine O'Neill Grace Harcourt Brace & Company (U.S. and Canada)

● Explains the training process for astronauts and support crew and tells readers how to get started on a career in space. Many information sources offered.

Design and Art Direction:
  Gordon Sibley Design Inc.
Editorial Director:
  Hugh Brewster
Project Editors:
  Ian R. Coutts, Mireille Majoor
Editorial Assistance:
  Susan Aihoshi, Laurie Coulter

Production Director:
  Susan Barrable
Production Co-ordinator:
  Donna Chong
Color Separation:
  Colour Technologies
Printing and Binding:
  Artegrafica S.p.A.

First on the Moon was produced by Madison Press Books, which is under the direction of Albert E. Cummings.